Full Access TO HOLLYWOOD'S BEST AND BRIGHTEST
BACKSTAGE PASS
HOLLYWOOD STARS

Mary Boone

TRIUMPH BOOKS

This book is available in quantity at special discounts for your group or organization. For further information, contact:

Triumph Books LLC
814 North Franklin Street
Chicago, Illinois 60610
Phone: (312) 337-0747
www.triumphbooks.com

Printed in U.S.A.

ISBN: 978-1-60078-901-4

Content developed and packaged by Rockett Media, Inc.
Writer: Mary Boone
Editor: Bob Baker
Design: Andrew Burwell
Page production: Chad Bell
Cover design by Andrew Burwell

Photographs courtesy of Getty Images unless otherwise noted

Full Access TO HOLLYWOOD'S BEST AND BRIGHTEST

BACKSTAGE PASS

HOLLYWOOD STARS

A hero from the post-apocalyptic nation of Panem. A coffee-drinking, poetry-reading 12-year-old boy. A kid whose best friend is a werewolf. A cancer patient who falls in love. What do all of these characters have in common? They're the stars of our favorite movies and TV shows, and you'll read all about them in *Backstage Pass: Hollywood Stars!*

From Jennifer Lawrence in *The Hunger Games* to Shailene Woodley in *Divergent* to Victoria Justice in the upcoming *Eye Candy,* girls are taking over movie theaters and our living rooms like never before.

They're talented, smart, confident, and ready to entertain us for years to come. But don't forget about the guys! Ansel Elgort starred with Shailene in *Divergent* and *The Fault in Our Stars,* and he stole our hearts in both films. Dylan O'Brien got his break on MTV's *Teen Wolf* and then starred in *The Maze Runner.* And despite losing the role of Thor to his brother, Chris, Liam Hemsworth has thrilled us as Gale in *The Hunger Games.*

In these pages, we profile 10 of the hottest television and movie actors in the business today. They've racked up hun-

Shailene Woodley and Ansel Elgort speak as 20th Century Fox presents The Fault in Our Stars *Soundtrack Event in Playa Vista, Calif.*

dreds of award nominations and won some pretty prestigious hardware, including a combined 19 Teen Choice Awards, 14 MTV Movie Awards, six Young Artists Awards, six Screen Actors Guild (SAG) Awards, six Young Hollywood Awards, two ALMA Awards and an Oscar. More importantly, they've made us laugh and cry and think. Here's to the young actors and actresses who light up our screens!

Zac Efron signs autographs at the world premiere of Neighbors in Los Angeles.

CHAPTER ONE

Zac Efron

As a pre-teen and teen, Zac Efron took music and acting lessons and was cast in some small television roles, but the California native never imagined he'd be able to make a living as an actor.

Then, he showed up at an open audition for a new Disney TV movie and everything changed.

"My mom dropped me off out of a mini-van somewhere in North Hollywood," he told *The Hollywood Reporter*. "I had no idea what to expect. There were about 40 guys. And we walked in, and (director) Kenny Ortega was there with a piano, and they put everybody in a room together, and we ran through different phases of what we would need to do – first dancing, then singing – and a few of us got tapped on the shoulder (to leave), and I didn't. And next came the scene-reading sections, and I got paired with Vanessa Hudgens."

His chemistry with Hudgens proved magical and became the foundation upon which Disney's *High School Musical* movie franchise was built (they also dated for a while, though he says they're no longer close). The "HSM" movies were such a

ALL ACCESS

Full name: Zachary David Alexander Efron

Birthdate: October 18, 1987

Birthplace: San Luis Obispo, Calif.

Early jobs: Zac started acting in local theater productions as a kid. In 2002, he landed guest roles on TV series, including *Firefly*, *ER* and *The Guardian*. In 2003, he was cast as a recurring character on the series *Summerland* and became a regular cast member in 2004.

Triumph: The young actor came under scrutiny when it was revealed that Drew Seeley provided the singing voice of Zac's *High School Musical* character. Some assumed Zac simply wasn't good enough but producers later revealed his voice was too low for the role. Zac did sing in *High School Musical 2* and *High School Musical 3*. He hasn't had a lot of singing roles lately, but he did star in the 2007 musical *Hairspray* – and, yes, that's really his voice.

Big break: In 2006, Zac gained fame as Troy Bolton in the Disney Channel original movie *High School Musical*.

Latest project: He starred in two 2014 theatrical releases: *That Awkward Moment* and *Neighbors*. He also lent his voice to the TV movie *Robot Chicken DC Comics Special II: Villains in Paradise*. His upcoming projects include the films *The Associate* and *We Are Your Friends*.

Website: www.zacefron.com

On Twitter: @ZacEfron

Twitter followers: 9.51 million

Reputation: Beautiful face, chiseled body, kind soul.

Why we love him: Have you looked into those blue, blue eyes?

huge hit that, in three short years, Disney produced a trio of them; it's estimated the films, soundtracks and accompanying merchandise generated more than $1 billion in revenues. Zac and his co-stars became overnight celebrities; they inspired video games, books, dolls and perfumes, while their images showed up on everything from T-shirts and lunch boxes to bedding and wall clocks.

Of course, critics are quick to dismiss teen stars, no matter how successful they may be. Actors including Lindsay Lohan, Miley Cyrus, Shia LaBeouf and Amanda Bynes are living proof that making the transition from child star to an adult career is difficult, especially if you want to keep your sanity intact.

This fact has forced Zac to work even harder and, despite a handful of box office bombs (*Charlie St. Cloud*, *The Paperboy*, *New Year's Eve* and *That Awkward Mo-*

ment), he has earned a solid reputation in the entertainment industry as a focused and versatile actor.

Burr Steers was the first director who gave Zac the chance to prove that he could carry a movie, casting him as a 37-year-old man in the body of a teenager in 2009's *17 Again*. In the movie, there's a scene that required Zac to spin a basketball on his fingers, while outsmarting the school bully. Steers says the young actor practiced the spinning "until his fingers were raw." The director told *Elle* magazine in April 2013: "Even the basketball wizards who were on set to train him couldn't believe that he could do that all day. He's really, really driven."

Director Lee Daniels openly admitted he didn't want to cast Zac in his 2012 movie *The Paperboy*, going so far as to call the young actor "corny." Daniels reluctantly met Zac and ultimately gave him the role

Zac Efron makes an appearance on MTV's Total Request Live.

of Jack Jansen, a young man who helps his brother prove the innocence of a man on death row.

"Zac was marvelous," Daniels told MTV in August 2012. "He was pure and hungry and eager to please and anxious to deliver the performance that he did. I'm really proud of what he did."

Some critics worry that Zac's effort to find his path as an adult actor has resulted in nonproductive meandering. He's tried his hand at musicals, family-friendly comedies, raunchy comedies, serious dramas, thrillers and small indie flicks.

Washington Post blogger Emily Yahr wrote in May 2014: "It's completely logical for Efron to try a bunch of different things. But by going in these short-lived phases, it simply makes him confusing to audiences — is he the rom-com guy? The frat bro? ... As of now, he still has fans that are willing to follow him anywhere, but at the moment he needs to pick a lane first so they'll know where to find him."

At the same time he's working to find his way professionally, Zac has endured personal struggles. In 2013, he felt his life was out of control. Nearly a year later, he talked about the experience while taping an episode of the ABC show *Running Wild with Bear Grylls*. The young actor said he was never stressed by work, but rather by

Zac Efron arrives for the premiere of the film At Any Price *at the 2012 Venice Film Festival.*

Zac Efron at the Oscars.

the times when he was "in-between work." He said he felt pressure everywhere he went because of the always watchful eye of the media.

"No matter who you are, you face challenges growing up," he said, noting that mistakes he made felt particularly humiliating because there were "so public and so scrutinized."

"When you have success young, and you accept the good things, you have to accept all of it. You have to accept the moments of glory, but also a great responsibility. And that responsibility, to some degree, involves being a role model," he told *The Hollywood Reporter*. "At the same time, I'm a human being, and I've made a lot of mistakes. I've learned from each one."

He said he's left the party scene behind and now strives to live an early-to-bed, early-to-rise lifestyle. He works out daily – swimming, rowing, lifting weights – and eats healthy foods, even drinking pH-balanced water from a specially installed faucet. He's made travel a priority and was thrilled to strengthen his relationship with his father during a 2013 trip to Peru.

Zac's career goals are also becoming more defined. Along with partner Michael Simkin, he's started producing through his company, Ninjas Runnin' Wild Productions. His first movie as producer, *That Awkward Moment*, was released in January 2014. He bought the rights to John Grisham's *The Associate*. His company's future projects also include two thrillers: *Fire* and *Black Math*.

"Believe me," Zac told *USA Today* in a summer 2014 interview, "if there is a moment in my life where everybody is pretty stoked about things, it's right now."

Bradley Cooper, left, and Zac Efron arrive at the Oscars.

CHAPTER TWO

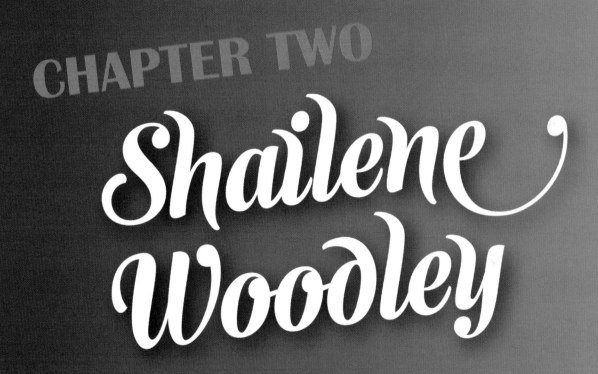

Shailene Woodley

When she was offered the role as Beatrice "Tris" Prior in the film trilogy *Divergent*, actress Shailene Woodley initially said, "*No thanks.*"

"I said 'no,' and everybody was shocked," she told *Teen Vogue* in early 2014. Then she sent an email to Katniss, looking for a little advice.

"I asked Jennifer Lawrence, 'Are you happy with your choice to take on *The Hunger Games*? And she said she wouldn't change it for the world. She told me, 'There are some things that you wouldn't want other people judging you for. But this is the best decision you'll ever make.'"

That nudge was all Shailene needed to change her mind. And, even though physical training was difficult, work days were long, and the film received mixed reviews, the young actress has no regrets.

"A big theme in my life is sisterhood," Shailene told *The Daily Beast*, "and I think that *Divergent* is a really great representation of that – of being there and supporting one another without the malicious attacks that so often come in movies and media. So many women feel so much anger toward other women."

The daughter of a school principal and guidance counselor, Shailene was just a toddler when she started modeling. She began acting in commercials by the time she was 5 and, after a handful of bit TV

Shailene Woodley poses for a portrait while promoting her 2013 film The Spectacular Now.

ALL ACCESS

Full name: Shailene Diann Woodley

Birthdate: November 15, 1991

Birthplace: Simi Valley, Calif.

Early jobs: She modeled as a preschooler and then, in 2002, Shailene landed small roles on the TV shows *Without a Trace* and *The District*. In 2005, she was nominated for a Young Artist Award for Best Leading Young Actress in a TV Movie, Miniseries or Special for her role in *A Place Called Home*.

Triumph: When she was 15, Shailene was diagnosed with Idiopathic Scoliosis and wore a chest-to-hips plastic brace for two years; the treatment proved successful.

Big break: Acting alongside superstar George Clooney in the 2011 film *The Descendants* earned Shailene both positive reviews and award nominations.

Latest project: She starred in 2014's *The Fault in Our Stars*, *Divergent* and *White Bird*. She's reprising her role as Tris in three additional installments in the *Divergent* series.

Website: shailene-woodley.org

On Twitter: @shailenewoodley

Twitter followers: 917,000

Reputation: She's an actress with a conscience.

Why we love her: Shailene redefines the label "carefree." While other stars help market expensive beauty products, this actress actually makes her own face scrubs, lotions and toothpaste.

Shailene Woodley arrives at the March 2014 world premiere of Divergent in Los Angeles.

roles, she was cast in *The Secret Life of the American Teenager* as Amy Juergens. Even after landing the starring role in the ABC Family series, Shailene continued to attend public high school, where she was a straight "A" student who sang in the choir and had an intense interest in the environment.

Shailene's star power grew exponentially thanks to her role as the daughter of George Clooney's character in the 2011 Oscar-winning film *The Descendants*. She won a Film Independent Spirit Award, an MTV Movie Award, and a Golden Globe nomination for her work as pouty teenager Alexandra King.

"After *The Descendants*, everybody was like, 'You've got to ride the wave!' And I was like, 'You ride the wave and it eventu-ally crashes on the shore. That doesn't work out! I'm going to just sit here and paddleboard,'" she told *Teen Vogue*. The California native read script after script, but nothing resonated with her for a full two years.

Being patient – and a little picky – paid off. Shailene scored starring roles in 2013's coming-of-age flick *The Spectacular Now* and in three 2014 releases: *Divergent*, *White Bird* and *The Fault in Our Stars*. (She also was cast as Mary Jane in *The Amazing Spider-Man 2* but her part was cut when the plot was reworked.)

Shailene's work as cancer-stricken Hazel Grace in *The Fault in Our Stars*, won raves from movie-goers and critics, many of whom called her performance "Oscar worthy."

"It is Ms. Woodley's movie at almost every moment she's on camera. She has the precious gift of simplicity, whether she's observing the people around her with a cool eye or filling the screen with a warmth that seems to come naturally. Others in the cast work at being winning; she wins by seeming to be herself. This young actress is the real, heart-piercing thing," wrote *Wall Street Journal* film critic Joe Morgenstern.

"Woodley ... has the gift of acting internally: she makes you watch her watch something, lets you read the mind of her character like a good book," wrote *Time's* Richard Corliss.

"After having the privilege of witnessing Shailene Woodley's transcendent, pure and authentic performance in *The Fault in Our Stars*, I believe there are now only four slots available in the category of Best Performance by An Actress in a Lead role. She's that memorable," gushed Richard Roeper in *The (Chicago) Sun-Times.*

While some young actors might sit back and revel in the glory of a successful year on the big screen, Shailene spent the summer of 2014 in Atlanta, shooting *Insurgent,* the second installment of the *Divergent* franchise. That film will hit theaters in March 2015. She's also committed to appear in the two-part finale of the franchise, *Allegiant* — *Part 1* and *Part 2,* to be released in early 2016 and 2017.

All these starring roles mean that walking the red carpet is now a regular part of Shailene's routine. But she refuses to portray herself as someone she's not, and has been known to attend premieres or awards shows in her comfy five-toed shoes or without any makeup at all.

"It's important because I saw somebody – what I thought was me – in a magazine once, and I had big red lips that definitely did not belong on my face," she told

Shailene Woodley is interviewed about her film The Spectacular Now *at the 2013 Sundance Film Festival.*

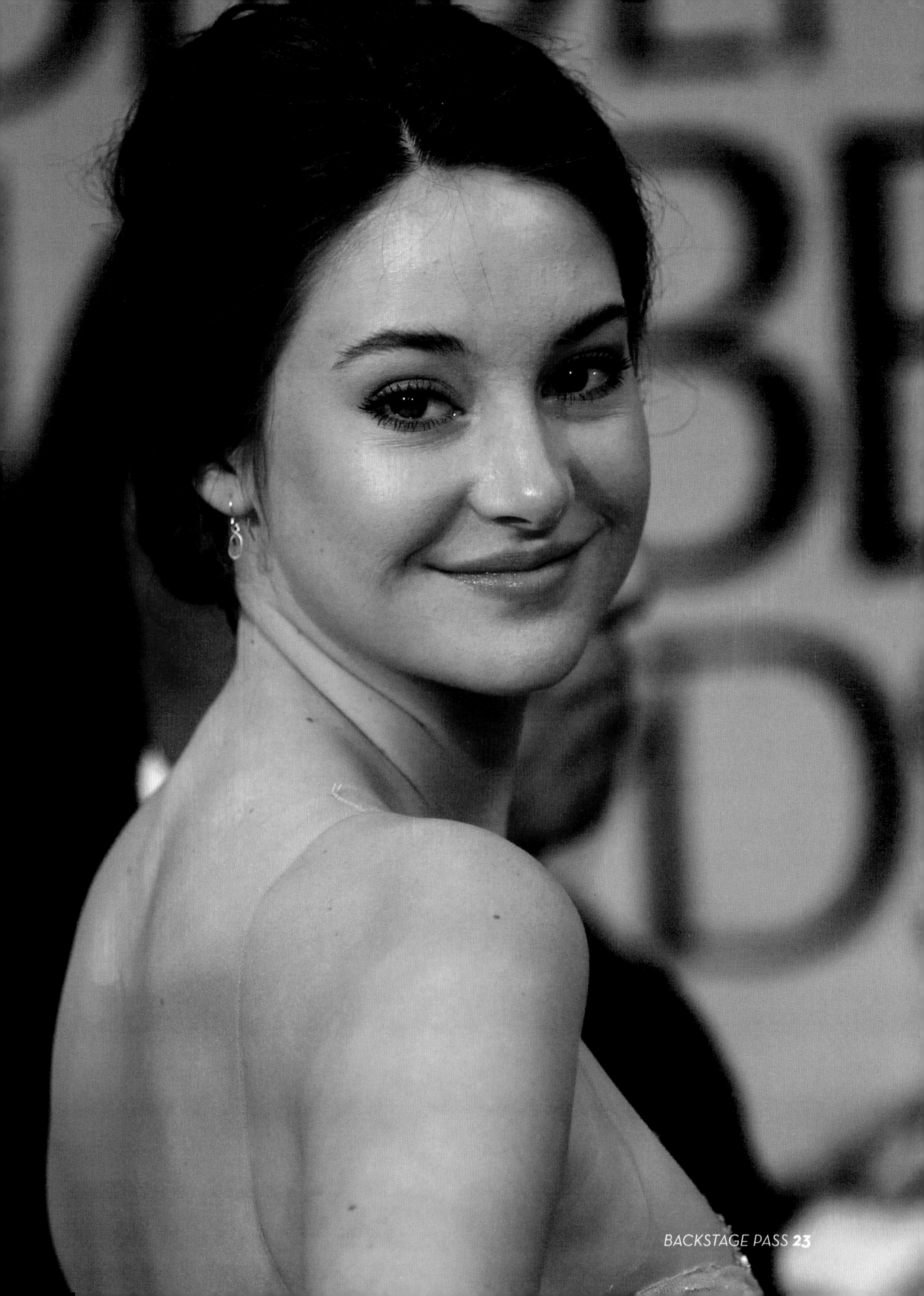

Shailene Woodley poses with her award for Favorite Character for Divergent at the 2013 MTV Movie Awards.

Interview magazine in 2014. "My stomach was completely flat. My skin was also flawless. But the reality is that I do not have those lips and my skin is not flawless and I do have a little bit of a stomach. It was not a proper representation of who I am. I realized that, growing up and looking at magazines, I was comparing myself to images like that, and most of it isn't real. So (a) I don't really wear makeup that much anyway, so part of it is just a selfish, lazy thing, and (b) I want to be me."

Beyond her authenticity, Shailene has also gained a reputation in the business as a big-time hugger. She embraces co-stars, directors, friends, fans and reporters alike, explaining to *The Hollywood Reporter* that a kind-hearted squeeze can break down barriers faster than almost anything. "We've got a set amount of time in our lives, you know. You might as well make every conversation count. So that's like the hug. It's kind of like, 'Hey, I'm real. You're real. Let's connect.'"

A unique combination of talent, sensibility and accessibility has helped this young actress win over a wide array of fans, among them her former co-star George Clooney. "Shailene can do whatever she wants," the two-time Oscar-winner told *Vanity Fair* in June 2014. "If she wants to be a movie star, she has it. If she wants to change the world, she will. Her talent and kindness go hand in hand."

Actress Shailene Woodley looks chic while attending a designer fashion show in Paris in October 2014.

CHAPTER THREE

Rico Rodriguez

It's hard to imagine anyone but Rico Rodriguez playing the role of espresso-sipping, poetry-reading, smoking jacket-wearing Manny Delgado on ABC's Emmy Award-winning comedy series *Modern Family*.

After all, becoming an actor wasn't even on his list of possibilities until his older sister, Raini, got into the business. She attended a talent association convention in Los Angeles in 2005, where she connected with manager Susan Osser. Soon after that, mom Diane moved to LA with Raini and Rico, while their father, Roy, stayed back in Texas, operating the family's tire shop.

The move was to be a one-year trial; if they didn't like it, Mom and the kids would go back home.

Of course, moving back to Texas never happened. Raini quickly landed small roles on television shows including *Huff, Handy Manny, Family of the Year, Parker* and *The Suite Life of Zack and Cody*. She's since become a regular on the TV show *Austin & Ally* and made her movie debut as Maya Blart in the feature film *Paul Blart: Mall Cop*.

Rico says he initially had no interest in acting, but that changed when, as a 6-year-old, he visited his sister on set and saw

Rico Rodriguez supports the Girl Scouts' #LetsGetHerToCamp campaign at the Teen Choice Awards.

ALL ACCESS

Full name: Rico Rodriguez

Birthdate: July 31, 1998

Birthplace: Bryan, Texas

Early jobs: Rico hadn't even considered becoming an actor until 2005, when his older sister, Raini, got into the business. He enrolled in acting classes and, before long, he was landing commercials. Small television roles came next, with guest spots on shows including *Jimmy Kimmel Live, Cory in the House, 'Til Death, ER, Nip/Tuck* and *iCarly.*

Identity crisis: When you talk about your love for Rico Rodriguez, you'll want to make sure you specify exactly which Rico you admire. Other entertainers who share the name include a Jamaica-born reggae trombonist, former drummer for the California rock band Picture Atlantic, and a fictional character from the video game Just Cause.

Big break: Rico was among nearly 200 kids who auditioned for the role of Manny on the ABC series *Modern Family.* He and his castmates have since won five consecutive Emmy awards for "Best Comedy Series."

Latest project: Alongside actor Efren Ramirez, he stars in *Endgame*, an independent film slated for release in 2014. Rico portrays a young boy who joins his school chess team and, thanks to his coach (Ramirez) "embarks on a journey of self-discovery, team spirit and the importance of family."

On Twitter: @StarringRico

Twitter followers: 303,000

Reputation: He's smart, enthusiastic and more mature than most his age.

Why we love him: He knows he's living the dream and he doesn't take it for granted.

how much fun she was having.

"When I told my mom I wanted to be an actor, she wanted me to be sure, because I change my mind a lot," Rico told Backstage. com in March 2011. "One day I want to be a NASCAR driver, one day I want to be an astronaut. But I actually stuck with this."

Rico enrolled in commercial and theatrical acting classes and, within about six months, he was ready for his first audition. "Fun fact," he told Backstage, "I didn't book that first job, but I booked the next three."

He landed roles in commercials for companies including Round Table Pizza, Time Warner Cable, Walmart and Dodge. Soon he'd also gotten his first TV role: a bit part on Disney Channel's *Corey in the House*. More small roles followed. Rico got small speaking parts on TV series including *ER, My Name is Earl* and *Nip/Tuck*.

Then, Rico auditioned for the part of Manny, a role he says he knew he was destined to play.

"I went in with different mindsets," he told *Popeater* in December 2010. "I never thought Manny would be how he is today. Then the producers told me, 'Think Antonio Banderas in a 12-year-old kid's body,' and I said, 'Oh, okay!' I went back, and I rocked it!"

"Rocked it" may be an understatement. Jeff Greenberg, the show's casting director, said of the 190 actors who auditioned for the part, Rico was both distinctive and impressive. "He was just very real and funny, and he has a great look," Greenberg told Backstage. "He says these sophisticated lines with that innocent face, and it's

beyond hilarious."

Rico skillfully portrays Manny as an extraordinarily debonair and chivalrous teenager. While fans often assume Rico and Manny are one and the same, Rico insists they're different in many ways. "I don't drink coffee," he told *Time Out New York* in 2011. "I don't write poems. I don't give flowers to girls ... yet. What I do have in common with him is that I have five nieces and one nephew. And I'm also a momma's boy. I really love my mom. And you too, Dad!"

His affection for his family is just one of many themes Rico discussed in his 2012 book *Reel Life Lessons ... So Far*. He also wrote about life with his TV family, specifically his on-screen mom, actress Sofia Vergara, who is quick to offer him motherly advice and sneak him handfuls of her favorite candies: Hot Tamales and marshmallows.

"In my eyes, I have two wonderful moms," he writes in his memoir. "Both amazing women who love me very much. That makes me so lucky."

While home schooling and taping *Modern Family* take up the majority of Rico's time these days, he's been able to squeeze in a few additional projects. For example, he stars alongside actor Efren Ramirez (*Napolean Dynamite*) in *Endgame*, an independent film scheduled for release in late 2014. Rico portrays a young boy who joins his school chess team and, thanks to his coach (Ramirez), "embarks on a journey of self-discovery, team spirit and the importance of family."

Rico also worked alongside producer

Edward James Olmos, director Richardo Arnaiz and actress Lisa Kudrow on the 3D animated film *El Americano*. The film tells the story of a pre-teen parrot (Rico) who flies from Mexico to the United States to enlist the aid of his favorite superhero. *El Americano* is the first major animated co-production between studios in Mexico and the United States, and is set to be released in theaters in spring 2015.

Rico says he'd like to continue working in the entertainment industry for years to come, either as an actor or behind the scenes, as an editor, director, producer or writer.

Wherever his future takes him, Rico plans to give it his all.

"My mom and dad always told me, 'Do your best. Don't expect to put in 50 percent and get 100 percent back. You need to put in 110 percent and you'll get 110 percent back,'" he told Backstage. "They always tell me that, to this day. And it's true: You have to put your best effort in. Fortunately for me, *Modern Family* has been my best effort. I really wanted it, and I work for it, and right now I am living the dream."

Rico Rodriguez arrives at Hub Network's 2013 Halloween Bash in Santa Monica, Calif.

*Rico and Raini Rodriguez
attend the 20th Annual
Screen Actors Guild Awards.*

CHAPTER FOUR

Dylan O'Brien

It worked for Justin Bieber and Carly Rae Jepsen, so why not Dylan O'Brien too?

Hoping to gain some editing experience and have a little fun, Dylan created his own YouTube channel called "Dis Be My Channel" back in 2006. The budding star posted videos showcasing his acting skills and sense of humor. Some of the more memorable clips showed him saying a tearful goodbye to the family's Christmas tree, avoiding studying for the SAT, and lip-syncing to the Spice Girls hit song "Wannabe."

Dylan says he had no intentions of becoming an actor when he produced those videos but they are, in fact, what led to him being discovered. Really.

In late 2009 he landed a role in a web series called *Sweety*, which was shown on sweetyhigh.com. While working on that mildly successful comedy, he met an actor who sent his videos to a management company. Dylan eventually signed with that company and – bam – he auditioned for and won a role on MTV's *Teen Wolf*.

Being on camera wasn't really in Dylan's

Dylan O'Brien participates in the Teen Wolf *panel at Comic-Con.*

ALL ACCESS

Full name: Dylan O'Brien

Birthdate: August 26, 1991

Birthplace: New York City, New York

Early jobs: In 2011, he won the role of "Stiles" Stilinski on MTV's supernatural drama *Teen Wolf*. In July 2014, MTV renewed the show for its fifth season.

Family business: Dylan is no stranger to the entertainment industry: his father, Patrick, is a cinematographer and his mother, Lisa, is a former actress who ran an acting school.

On another note: Dylan used to play drums in an all-male band called Slow Kids at Play. In an August 2014 interview with *Entertainment Weekly*, he described the group's sound as "pop-punk elements but more of the beachy, reggae vibe."

Big break: *Teen Wolf* really was Dylan's big break – he'd done next to nothing before landing that gig. Still, after just a handful of episodes, it was clear he had star potential.

Latest project: Dylan's big mainstream break, *The Maze Runner*, was released in September 2014. In the science fiction action thriller, based on James Dashner's 2009 book of the same name, Dylan plays 16-year-old Thomas who wakes up in a rusty elevator with no memory of who he is, only to learn he's been delivered to the middle of an intricate maze, along with a slew of other boys, who have been trying to find their way out of the ever-changing labyrinth.

On Twitter: @dylanobrien

Twitter followers: 2.1 million

Reputation: Quirky heartthrob

Why we love him: He loves his co-stars, he loves his fans, he loves life.

plans and, as flattered as he is to have ended up there, he's still a little uncomfortable watching himself on screen.

"I wanted to make movies, (maybe become) a director because my dad is a cinematographer," he told KidzWorld.com in 2012. "But personal performance for me was a problem as a kid. I played music and hated to perform in front of people. That was a hurdle for me, so I never thought I could act. I thought behind the camera was where I belonged."

Dylan says he struggled with his timing and delivery during the early days of *Teen Wolf.*

"You watch the pilot of *Teen Wolf* and I'm a different actor today," he told KidzWorld. "I was very green then and more nervous and less aware."

Over the course of four seasons, Dylan has grown enormously as an actor and his show has evolved into an award-winning thriller. Much of the show's allure centers around the friendship between Dylan's character Stiles and his friend, teen wolf Scott McCall, played by Tyler Posey. Off screen, the actors are real-life pals who hang out at each others' houses, play video games together, and have gotten to know each others' parents.

As he's stretched his acting wings, Dylan has taken on a couple of film roles. He played the school-skipping neighbor kid in 2011's improvised comedy *High Road* and starred alongside Victoria Justice in 2012's romantic comedy *The First Time.*

In 2013, he landed a role in *The Internship,* a comedy that tells the story of Billy (Vince Vaughn) and Nick (Owen Wilson), fired salesmen who try to prove they're still relevant by getting internships at Google alongside a bunch of super smart college students. Dylan's character, Stuart, comes off as a bit of a jerk, especially when it comes to interacting with the film's stars.

"That was intimidating at first," he told *Just Jared Jr.* in 2013. "I was so afraid, like 'Oh my God, I don't know if I'm going to be able to pull this off.' The whole dynamic I established with Vince was that I was just this jerk to him. And I was like, 'Are people going to buy that?' But yeah, it was so much fun."

After just a handful of movie roles, landing a major role in *The Maze Runner* was anything but a sure thing. Dylan auditioned and met with the casting director but says he'd nearly given up hope when he didn't hear back for about six weeks.

Director Wes Ball admits his initial reaction was that Dylan was too "cool" to play the movie's innocent lead.

"It took me a lot of time to talk to Dylan, to just get to know him and understand that he can do the very emotional, soft, nuanced stuff," Ball told Reuters news service in September 2014.

Blame it on the hair, jokes Dylan. "Wes was like, 'His hair is too MTV,'" Dylan told Collider.com. "That's what he thought, which was so funny. Then he saw a picture of me with more regular hair, the buzz-cut or something from *Teen Wolf,* and he brought me back and it worked. It just ended up working out."

Actually it "worked out" in a big way.

Over its debut weekend, the movie, based on James Dashner's novel of the same name, brought in an estimated $32.5 million of its $34 million production budget. Even before the debut weekend ended, 21st Century Fox announced plans for a sequel; *The Maze Runner: Scorch Trials* is scheduled for release in September 2015.

Dylan says he and his character, Thomas, share some of the same characteristics, particularly when it comes to their good-intentioned rebellious streaks.

"I've always been the same way," he told Teen.com in August 2014.

"I have different ways of thinking. I'm not shy about them either. And that could sometimes strike people in a certain way. Like when you're adamant about what you believe in, but I've always been that way and that's something that's really primal in Thomas as well, so I think that's why I can play it, or relate to it and understand him."

Dylan, who has already won a Giffoni Award, Teen Choice Award and Young Hollywood Award, gets a little defensive when critics constantly compare *The Maze Runner* to other post-apocalyptic young adult films – specifically *The Hunger Games* and *Divergent*. The three are very different, very distinctive stories, he insists.

"We don't have romance in (*The Maze Runner*) and I love that, for the first time in one of these really cool YA stories," he told *The Hollywood Reporter* in September 2014. "During what's going on (in the other films), how is there romance happening? It doesn't make any sense – these kids are fighting for their lives, they're not gonna stop and kiss and cuddle, and I love that so much (about *The Maze Runner*.) It's so not YA, it's a sci-fi action thriller."

You tell 'em, Dylan!

Dylan O'Brien participates in The Maze Runner *panel at the 2013 Comic-Con.*

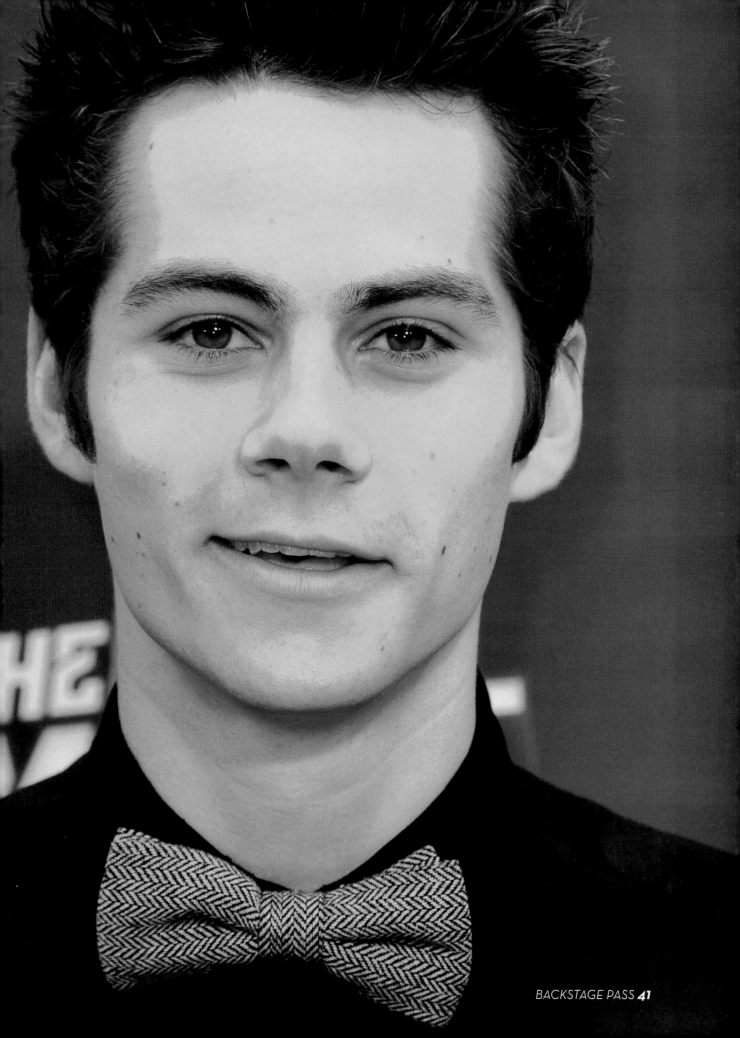

CHAPTER FIVE

Ansel Elgort

New York native Ansel Elgort got his first taste of performing when he was just 9 years old.

"I did ballet and I went out on stage for the first time as a ballet dancer and I liked being on stage and then later that turned into wanting to be an actor," he told *Parade* magazine in May 2014.

His appetite whetted, Ansel kept practicing his craft, eventually enrolling in New York's famed Fiorello H. LaGuardia High School of Music & Art and Performing Arts. "I always did workshops. I would be at theater camp, doing shows, or after-school programs. Then I was doing shows in school. It was nonstop," he told *Interview* magazine in 2014. "I was never *not* in a show from ages 11 until 18. It was a great creative atmosphere but also a professional kind of atmosphere. When I finally went into the professional world, I felt ready. I was prepared for work."

Ansel, the son of a fashion photographer father and opera director mother, landed his first professional acting job while he was still in high school. He played the role of an 18-year-old outsider with a secret in the off-Broadway play *Regrets*.

Men, Women & Children actor Ansel Elgort answers questions from the media during the Toronto International Film Festival.

ALL ACCESS

Full name: Ansel Elgort

Birthdate: March 14, 1994

Birthplace: New York City, NY

Early jobs: Ansel began his professional acting career in the 2012 off-Broadway play, *Regrets*, by Matt Charman. Reviews of his performance were not exactly flattering. *New York Times* critic Charles Isherwood wrote: "Mr. Elgort is stiffer than his crisp blue jeans in the crucial role of Caleb. Hitching his thumbs into his pockets and striking (James) Dean-like poses, he looks the model of a handsome but troubled 1950s youth, but brings absolutely no spark or suggestion of inner life to the role."

Music Man: Under the name "Ansølo," Ansel is also an electronic dance music producer. He released his first record, *Unite*, in April 2014. "My style is clubby and groovy," he told *The Hollywood Reporter* in March 2014. "You can jump to it, but you don't just have to just jump to it. It's not just really bass-heavy and hurts your ears; you move with it, and it sounds kind of tribal."

Big break: He was strictly a theater kid until he landed the part of Tommy Ross in the 2013 remake of the horror movie *Carrie*.

Latest project: Ansel starred in 2014 movies: *Divergent*, *The Fault in Our Stars* and *Men, Women & Children*. *The Divergent Series: Insurgent* is due out in 2015 and he's been signed to play the title role in *Van Cliburn*.

On Twitter: @AnselElgort

Twitter followers: 2.02 million

Reputation: Co-star Shailene Woodley calls him "a nugget of light." Now, that's a reputation.

Why we love him: He's charming in a way that makes him appealing to both teens and their parents.

Actor Ansel Elgort poses at the premiere of Men, Women & Children at Ryerson Theatre during the 2014 Toronto International Film Festival.

"I think my age helped," he told the *(New York) Daily News* during a 2012 interview about winning his first big role. He also noted that high school history classes proved valuable to understanding the show's 1950s setting.

Shortly after graduation, Ansel landed his first film role in the 2013 remake of the horror flick *Carrie* alongside actresses Chloe Grace Moretz and Julianne Moore.

"With *Carrie*, I did like seven auditions," he told *The Hollywood Reporter* in 2014. "I'd never done a movie, so they wanted to make sure I wasn't going to ruin it. I don't blame them."

Carrie got mixed reviews but critics overwhelmingly praised Ansel's work in the film. *The (Toronto) Star*'s Bruce DeMara wrote that Ansel "does fine work as doomed golden boy Tommy Ross." Gary Dowell wrote in the *Lake Highlands (Texas) Advocate* that Ansel was "well cast" in the role and Tim Robey of *The (London) Telegraph* called him the movie's "surprising stand-out."

Shortly after wrapping up shooting on *Carrie*, Ansel went in search of more work – and he found plenty.

He landed the role of Caleb Prior in the film adaptation of the dystopian sci-fi book *Divergent*, which was released in March 2014. Then, *The Fault in Our Stars*, based on John Green's best-selling young adult novel, hit theaters in the June 2014. His portrayal of cancer-stricken amputee Gus sealed his fate as a superstar and earned him a Young Hollywood Award, an MTV Millennial Award, and four Teen Choice Awards, including Choice Movie Actor Drama, Choice Movie Breakout Star and Choice Liplock.

The hotter-than-hot actor also stars alongside Jennifer Garner, Judy Greer and Adam Sandler in *Men, Women & Children*, a fall 2014 release based on a novel of the same name written by author Chad Kultgen. He's finished filming *The Divergent Series: Insurgent*, due out in March 2015 and he's been signed to play piano virtuoso Harvey Lavan "Van" Cliburn, Jr. in *Van Cliburn*, a biopic based on the novel by Howard Reich.

Actress Shailene Woodley, who played his sister in *Divergent* and his love interest in *The Fault in Our Stars*, is a big fan of her co-star.

"Every single day (Ansel) looks at the world with a new set of eyes," she told *People* magazine in June 2014. "He is the most creative person I've ever met. This dude is a producer. He paints miniatures and wins contests painting miniatures, which is insane. He's a ballet dancer. He is literally the most creative person."

Most creative person? Humble Ansel blushes at the compliment, instead preferring labels like "quirky" and "weird." He forgoes hip hobbies like surfing and skateboarding in favor of painting tiny Warhammer figurines. He owns his own ballet and tap shoes and he's proud of his mastery of music sequencer software – heck, he's produced his own electronic music under the name "Ansølo."

So, how has this self-professed "sexy book nerd" managed to snag such impressive roles so quickly?

"Even my agents and everyone are sort of saying that you're not supposed to get them," he told *The Hollywood Reporter*. "They've never really had anyone who's done this really quickly. I guess it would have to be that I did a lot of stage first. I've been performing and working for a while. I put a lot of work into it. It was really non-stop for years."

Ansel, whose fans call themselves "Anselites," isn't about to take his newfound fame for granted. He's grateful for the opportunities but also mildly wary.

"You get a million messages from people you've never met, and people you haven't talked to in years saying, 'Hey man, let's hang out and catch up,'" he told the *New York Post* in March 2014. "And I'm like, 'I don't know you, nor do I want to catch up with you.' You have to be out of that bubble a little bit."

While he's happy to read scripts and attend premieres for now, Ansel isn't willing to commit to acting only for the rest of his career. He has too many other talents and interests he wants to pursue.

"I don't just act, and that's really important to me," he told *Interview* magazine. "I don't want to just be an actor forever. Right now I'm really into music. I want to score movies. I could be an actor first, but I don't only want to be an actor."

Ansel Elgort signs autographs at the Divergent world premiere in Los Angeles.

Ansel Elgort accepts his
Teen Choice surfboard
award for Choice Movie
Actor Drama for his role in
The Fault in Our Stars.

CHAPTER SIX
Elle Fanning

Elle Fanning has accomplished a lot in a very short time. The Georgia-born actress turns 17 in April 2015. She's already been in show business for 15 years and has made nearly two dozen movies.

Family ties helped Elle land her first roles. As a toddler, she got a bit part in the 2001 Sean Penn movie *I Am Sam*, portraying the younger version of sister Dakota Fanning's character. Similarly, she got a role in Steven Spielberg's Emmy Award-winning science fiction mini-series *Taken*. At age 4, Elle landed her first role independent of her sister in the comedy *Daddy Day Care*.

And the parts kept coming. She was cast in the small role of Sweetie Pie Thomas in 2003's *Because of Winn-Dixie*. In 2004, she worked with Jeff Bridges and Kim Basinger in *The Door in the Floor* and did voice work for the English version of the Japanese animated film *My Neighbor Totoro*. Then came roles in *I Want Someone to Eat Cheese With*, *Babel*, *The Nines*, *Déjà Vu*, and TV's *The Lost Room* and *House: MD*.

By late 2006, Elle was landing lead roles; her first came in the drama *Reserva-*

Elle Fanning arrives at a Paris Fashion show in March 2014.

ALL ACCESS

Full name: Mary Elle Fanning

Birthdate: April 9, 1998

Birthplace: Conyers, Georgia

Early jobs: Elle was just 18 months old when she played the younger version of Dakota Fanning's character in the movie *I Am Sam*. In 2002, when she was 4, Fanning won her first role independent of her sister in the Eddie Murphy comedy *Daddy Day Care*.

Royalty: Historians have discovered Elle is the 22nd great-granddaughter of England's King Edward III. Michelle Ercanbrack, a family historian for Ancestry.com, told *People* magazine in 2014 that connection means Elle and Kate Middleton, Duchess of Cambridge, are distant cousins. "You can consider her a long-lost princess," Ercanbrack said of Elle. "This connection is so unique and rare."

Big break: Elle began to book lead roles by the end of 2006. The first of these was the part of Emma Learner in the drama *Reservation Road*. She played the grieving daughter of Grace and Ethan Learner; the film tells the story of the aftermath of a tragic car accident in which Emma's brother is killed. Critics really took notice of the young actress thanks to her scene-stealing appearance in 2008's *Super 8*.

Latest project: Elle provided the voice for a 9-year-old girl named Winnie in the animated film *The Boxtrolls* and starred in the science fiction film *Young Ones*; both films were released in late 2014. She's also signed on to play Mary Shelley in upcoming movie *A Storm In The Stars*.

Social media: Not this girl. No Twitter, no Facebook. Yes, there are accounts out there, but Elle insists they're all fake.

Reputation: Sunny, smart, talented.

Why we love her: Sure, she's super beautiful and super famous, but she's still so authentic and sweet and normal.

tion Road. She starred alongside Joaquin Phoenix and Jennifer Connelly in the film about dealing with the aftermath of a tragic car accident. In 2007, she got a small part in *The Curious Case of Benjamin Button*, the title role in *Phoebe in Wonderland*, and the role of Mary in *The Nutcracker in 3D*. In 2010, she appeared in the drama *Somewhere*, written and directed by Sofia Coppola and later as a ghost in *Twixt*, a film written by Francis Ford Coppola.

Elle really captured critics' attention with her performance as Alice in 2011's *Super 8*. *Rolling Stone*'s Peter Travers wrote: "Fanning delivers a shooting-star performance that takes you places you don't see coming," *The Denver Post*'s Lisa Kennedy reported: "When Alice isn't onscreen, *Super 8* becomes less super," and *Entertainment Weekly*'s Lisa Schwarzbaum called Elle "extraterrestrially talented." The reviews were a boost to a career that was already in high gear and led to even bigger roles in higher profile films.

In December 2011, Elle appeared alongside Scarlett Johansson in *We Bought a Zoo*. In September 2012, she starred as Ginger in the widely acclaimed drama *Ginger & Rosa*. In early 2014, she starred with John Hawkes and Glenn Close in the drama *Low Down*. She then played dreamy Princess Aurora in *Maleficent*. Based upon the 1959 animated classic *Sleeping Beauty*, the updated movie explores the untold story of the enchanted forest and gave Elle a chance to co-star with Angelina Jolie, who played the wicked fairy.

"To say I'm Aurora is still so weird – I

have to keep pinching myself," Elle told *The New York Post* in May 2014. "She was my favorite because I felt like I looked like her the most – the blond hair and the pink dress, and she's the tallest princess, so that worked out really well."

As far as working with superstar Jolie goes, Elle readily admits she was initially intimidated but that anxiety disappeared the second the two met.

"She gave me a huge hug and she took my shoulders and said, 'We are going to have the best time working together,'" Elle told *Teen Vogue* in 2014. "And we did. We had the best time."

Elle has been very intentional in her selection of roles, not wanting to be typecast. That's evidenced by her most recent roles – all of which are vastly different. In *The Boxtrolls,* an animated movie released in September 2014, she voiced a snarky, pampered 9-year-old named Winnie. In *Young Ones*, released a month later, she portrayed a teen facing a bleak future when her desolate future society runs out of water.

"I try to do very different roles," she told *Elle* magazine in 2014. "It's fun to go from something like *Maleficent* to something more independent, and mix it up in that way. It would be fun to play a darker role. I felt like with Winnie I was excited because I'd never played someone like that before – someone so spoiled."

Elle's next project will see her starring in the indie film *A Storm in the Stars*. The period drama centers on the love affair of 17-year-old poet Percy Shelley and 17-year-old Mary Wollstonecraft, who later wrote *Frankenstein* under the pen name Mary Shelley. Filming is expected to begin in 2015.

When she's not filming movies, Elle lives a life that's as normal as possible, often recalling the advice given to her by four-time Oscar nominee Annette Bening. "When we did *Ginger & Rosa* together, she wanted to make sure I was having a normal teenage life," Elle said in a 2014 interview. "She said, 'Make sure you take time and you don't work too much and you still go to your prom.' And I have. I always remember that she said that because it is important and it is what I want."

Elle attends a regular high school, takes ballet classes and loves reading fashion magazines. Even though she walks the red carpet, attends movie premieres and admits to regular email correspondence with Scarlett Johansson, she doesn't think she's all that different from other kids her age.

"Some people do piano lessons after school; I do movies," she told *Teen Vogue* in January 2014.

While Elle and Dakota are undeniably close, Dakota says she's careful not to advise her younger sister about professional matters.

"I always know what she's filming and where she is and who she's working with, but I don't give her advice on it," Dakota told *Teen Vogue* in June 2014. "We both have our own paths that we're confident in, so she's never asked me. Of course I'd tell her if she wanted me to, but I also think that choosing the films that you want to do is a really personal thing — it's kind of just a feeling that you get and you're the only person who understands it."

Elle Fanning attends the world premiere of The Twilight Saga: Breaking Dawn Part II *at Los Angeles' Nokia Theatre.*

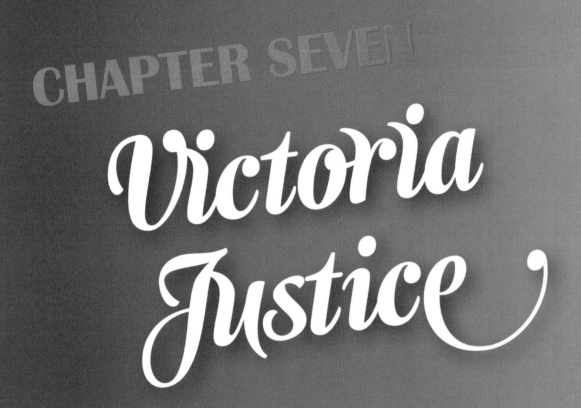

CHAPTER SEVEN

Victoria Justice

Not everyone can say their career was inspired by a chip commercial, but Victoria Justice can.

The Hollywood, Florida, native recalls that she was just 8 years old when she saw an advertisement on TV that made her hungry for more than just junk food. "I was like, 'Mom, I can do that,'" she told *Interview* magazine in 2012. Convinced to at least give her daughter a taste of the fame she desired, Victoria's mother took her to a South Beach modeling agency.

Turns out, Victoria wasn't the only one who thought she'd be a natural in front of the camera. Very soon, she was booking jobs. She did a commercial for Ovaltine malted milk and began appearing in print ads for clothiers Polo Ralph Lauren and H&M. At age 10, she won a walk-on role in an episode of the WB's comedy-drama *Gilmore Girls*.

Buoyed by Victoria's early success, her family moved to Hollywood, California, in 2003. Shortly after that, she auditioned for and was accepted into the musical theater program at Millikan Performing Arts Academy, a performing arts magnet school in Los Angeles. She continued to do commercial work and landed a guest role on the Disney Channel series *The Suite Life of Zack & Cody* and cameos on *iCarly* and *Everwood*. The young actress won a role in the 2005 drama *Mary*. The film, which was not widely released, premiered at the

Victoria Justice arrives at the Kids' Choice Awards in March 2013.

ALL ACCESS

Full name: Victoria Dawn Justice

Birthdate: February 19, 1993

Birthplace: Hollywood, Florida

Early jobs: Victoria's first theatrical role was unglamorously credited as "Jill No. 2" during a 2003 guest appearance on the WB comedy-drama series *Gilmore Girls*. Within a year, she'd also landed a guest role on The Disney Channel's popular comedy *The Suite Life of Zack & Cody*.

Big break: In 2005, she won a major role in the Nickelodeon series *Zoey 101*, working alongside actress Jamie Lynn Spears. That same year, she earned roles in three movies: the drama-thriller *Mary*, the comedy *When Do We Eat?* and the Hallmark television film *Silver Bells*.

Representing: Victoria's mom is Puerto Rican and her dad is of English, German, Irish ancestry. The actress is proud of her ancestry and thinks it makes her unique in Hollywood. "I think that ... a lot of role models that kids have usually aren't Hispanic," she told the website Mom.me in 2013. "I think it's really cool that I can represent that sort of melting pot. I think that Latina girls and even guys need to be able to look up to someone who's similar to them on TV, and I think that's really cool that I could be able to do that and that they can relate to me."

Latest project: Victoria landed the lead role in MTV's new drama series *Eye Candy,* based on R.L. Stine's *(Goosebumps)* best-seller and stars in the movie *The Outskirts*. Oh, and she's recording music too. Though she parted ways with her label in August 2014, Victoria still hopes to release her debut album in 2015.

Twitter: @VictoriaJustice

Twitter followers: 8.4 million

Reputation: Talented, down to earth, polite.

Why we love her: She's gorgeous, she's talented and she loves a good prank – just ask her *Victorious* cast mates or the guys in Big Time Rush.

Venice Film Festival where it won a special jury prize.

Things were happening for Victoria – and happening fast.

In mid-2005, she joined the cast of the popular Nickelodeon TV series *Zoey 101*, portraying Lola Martinez, a new student who loves acting. Victoria also had roles in other films that year: the comedy *When Do We Eat?* and the Hallmark TV movie *Silver Bells*. Her newfound fame brought with it red carpet opportunities and magazine cover shoots – which led to even more fame. In 2006, she earned a supporting role in the thriller *The Garden*.

While still filming *Zoey 101*, Victoria began recording music; her first single was released in mid-2007. With music clearly in her blood, she guest starred on an episode of Nickelodeon's series *The Naked Brothers Band*. In 2009, she starred and performed three songs in the Nickelodeon musical, *Spectacular!* The film still ranks as one of Nickelodeon's most popular movies, attracting an audience of 3.7 million on its premiere night.

Taking notice of Victoria's many talents and popularity, Nickelodeon made her the star of her own show, *Victorious*, in 2010. In the show, Victoria's alter ego, Tori Vega, is an aspiring entertainer at an LA performing arts high school. The series, which aired through 2012 and showcased Victoria's vocals on its soundtrack releases, took home "Favorite TV Show" honors at both the 2012 and 2013 Nickelodeon Kids' Choice Awards.

While she's grateful for her start in kids' and teen programming, Victoria is anxious to gracefully transition to more mature

Victoria Justice works to inspire kids in Harlem to read in her role as spokesperson for the Soar With Reading program.

roles. She considers herself equal parts actress and singer, and works hard to balance the two.

"I love writing music; it's just a great outlet and it's something that's very creative and fun for me," she told NewsOK.com in June 2013. "And I love performing. At the same time I also love playing different characters and being on set and learning from different actors and directors."

She took a lead role in 2010's *Fun Size*, in which she plays a snarky teen who takes her younger brother trick-or-treating and loses him. Musically, Victoria moved from TV soundtracks to headlining her first concert tour – alongside boy band Big Time Rush – in summer 2013. Though she parted ways with her label in August 2014, she still hopes to release her debut album in 2015.

Victoria landed the lead role in MTV's new drama series *Eye Candy*, based on the R.L. Stine bestseller; the show began airing in late 2014. She also will have two movies released in 2015: the indie romantic comedy, *Naomi + Ely's No Kiss List*, based on the young adult novel by Rachel Cohn and David Levithan, and her high school movie *The Outskirts*, in which she stars alongside Eden Sher from TV's *The Middle*.

No matter how bright Victoria's future may be, her mom, Serene Justice-Reed, said she's always been confident of Victoria's ability to handle fame. What worries her is the criticism that often accompanies that fame.

"Everything is judged and your family and friends become judged as well," Serene told *The Better Show*, a nationally syndicated lifestyle program, during a 2013 interview. "I just try to tell her 'Don't take it personally. Those people don't know you. Try not to read any comments or other things.'"

Victoria Justice arrives at the June 2014 premiere of Davis Guggenheim's documentary Spent: Looking for Change.

Victoria Justice attends at DKNY fashion show in New York City in February 2014.

Victoria says she does occasionally check online forums to see what people are saying about her. The spunky entertainer admits negative comments can hurt her feelings but, rather than strike back, she prefers to live by more of her mom's advice: "Always treat people the way you'd like to be treated – she always says that."

Her mother's good counsel may be one of the reasons Victoria has been so devoted to charitable causes. She's been part of "Girl Up" since 2011, a United Nations Foundation campaign that focuses on protecting the rights of girls throughout the world. She also supports Aid Still Required, an organization that brings attention and humanitarian aid to areas suffering from natural disasters or human crises; AT&T's "It Can Wait" campaign, which encourages people not to text and drive; and DoSomething.org, a group that encourages young people to become involved in social causes. In 2014, she partnered with JetBlue to work on its "Soar with Reading" Program, an initiative aimed at encouraging kids to read and use their imaginations.

Victoria says she feels a responsibility to promote causes that go beyond red carpet glam.

"It's so important to spread a message of giving back to your community, and to the world," she told LookToTheStars.org. "Especially nowadays with this generation, having access to so much social media — Twitter, Facebook — there are so many ways to reach people: and spread awareness for whatever charity or cause you are passionate about. There are so many ways you can really make a difference."

Books and reading are important to Victoria Justice, who spends time reading aloud to kids in Harlem as part of JetBlue Airways' Soar with Reading event.

CHAPTER EIGHT

Chloe Grace Moretz

Sure, Chloe Grace Moretz is still a teenager, but she's also a show business veteran. The Atlanta native landed her first major movie role, in *The Amityville Horror,* when she was just 6. She's since acted in more than 30 films and a handful of TV shows, ranging from the Disney Channel's animated *My Friends Tigger & Pooh* to NBC's popular sitcom *30 Rock.*

With all those scripts to read, auditions to attend and scenes to tape, you'd think she missed out on childhood. Not so, says Chloe Grace, who told *The (London) Telegraph* in August 2013: "I've actually had a more interesting childhood because I've been able to travel the world and actually see the things I've learned in my history books first hand."

The daughter of a nurse and a plastic surgeon, Chloe Grace first became interested in acting thanks to her older brother Trevor. In 2002, Chloe and her mother moved with Trevor to New York City so that he could attend the Professional Performing Arts High School.

Trevor studied at the school for two years; then the entire family, including Chloe Grace, her father and three older brothers, moved to Los Angeles so Trevor could pursue his dreams. Chloe Grace helped her brother learn lines and he reciprocated by sharing some of the lessons he'd learned in acting classes. It was an

Chloe Grace Moretz arrives on the red carpet at the 2014 Much Music Video Awards in Toronto.

ALL ACCESS

Full name: Chloe Grace Moretz

Birthdate: February 10, 1997

Birthplace: Atlanta, Georgia

Early jobs: Chloe's first-ever part came on CBS' drama series *The Guardian*.

Big break: Chloe's first big role came in the 2005 remake of *The Amityville Horror*. She portrayed Chelsea, a young girl whose family moves into a house where the previous owner had murdered his family. She received a Young Artist Award nomination for her work in the film.

Not Katniss: It's hard to imagine anyone other than Jennifer Lawrence portraying Katniss in *The Hunger Games* movie franchise, but Chloe Grace was also among the finalists for the job. "Yeah, I read all of the books," she told the *Los Angeles Times* back in January 2011. The then-13-year-old said enthusiastically at the time, "I'd die to play Katniss. It's such a cool role." Her career seems to have fared alright, in spite of not landing that particular role.

Latest project: The multi-faceted actress starred in six movies in 2014: *Muppets Most Wanted, Laggies, Clouds of Sils Maria, If I Stay, The Equalizer, The Tale of Princess Kaguya* and *Dark Places*. She's already hard at work on Sony Picture's *The Fifth Wave*, a film adaptation of Rick Yancey's novel, scheduled for release in 2016.

Twitter: @ChloeGMoretz

Twitter followers: 1.24 million

Reputation: She's a "good girl" who is determined to avoid the pitfalls of fame.

Why we love her: Chloe is a self-proclaimed feminist who lets her personal views guide her career choices. "I never wanted to play into the stereotypes; I've always wanted to go against them in life in general," she told HuffingtonPost.com in September 2014. "My mom, I have to give her a lot of credit, because she raised me in that setting in real life. Art imitates life, and it just kind of bled into that."

Though the purple wig makes her nearly unrecognizable,* Chloe Grace Moretz won critical praise for her role in the 2010 movie Kick Ass.

exercise that piqued her interest in performing and soon found her auditioning for roles of her own.

Her first roles were small. She played the role of Violet, a neglected child, in two episodes of CBS' crime series *The Guardian*. Shortly after that, she made her movie debut in 2005's low-budget film *Heart of the Beholder*, which won five back-to-back Best Feature Film awards on the indie film festival circuit. Chloe Grace's appearance in the 2005 remake of *The Amityville Horror* earned her a Young Artist Award nomination and more roles; she got small parts in Martin Lawrence's movie *Big Momma's House 2* and TV shows including *Dirty Sexy Money*, *Desperate Housewives* and *My Friends Tigger & Pooh*.

If Chloe Grace's fame had been simmering before, it came to a full boil in 2010,

when she starred as the potty-mouthed, purple-wig-wearing Hit-Girl in Matthew Vaughn's comic-book film *Kick-Ass*. The film's over-the-top violence drew criticism, but Chloe Grace received widespread critical acclaim for her performance. Film critic Roger Ebert wrote: "Say what you will about her character, but Chloe Grace Moretz has presence and appeal."

Over the years, the roles have kept coming, each more different than the last. She played a seventh grader who works for the school newspaper in *Diary of a Wimpy Kid*, a damsel in distress in *Jack and the Beanstalk*, an abused girl in the crime thriller *Texas Killing Fields*, the spunky sidekick in Martin Scorsese's *Hugo*, and a rebellious teenager in Tim Burton's 2012 film *Dark Shadows*.

Most recently, she worked alongside

Chloe Grace Moretz signs autographs at the September 2014 premiere of The Equalizer.

Juliette Binoche and Kristen Stewart in the drama *Clouds of Sils Maria* and with Keira Knightley in the romantic comedy *Laggies*. She played the bullied-then-vengeful high school girl in an update of Stephen King's *Carrie* and befriended Denzel Washington's character, a retired black ops government operative, in *The Equalizer*.

"I think in a way, I blame my teenage mind for the diversity in my roles," the actress told film critic Tim Lammers in an August 2014 interview. "As a teenage girl, I can't really choose what to wear in the morning, and in the same way, I can't really choose what my next movie is going to be. I feel that's why my movie choices are all over the place. My emotions are changing every other month, so I think my movies change with me."

While some of Chloe Grace's recent roles have been fairly mature, she won favor with the teen crowd thanks to her role in 2014's *If I Stay*. Based on the bestselling young adult novel of the same name, the movie featured Chloe Grace as Mia Hall, a high school senior and gifted cellist who is on the road to musical greatness when a car crash kills her family and leaves her in a coma. Through an out-of-body experience, Mia recounts pivotal moments in her life, and is reminded through the whispers of an emergency room nurse that it's only her fight that will determine whether she lives or dies.

The young actress also made her off-Broadway debut as Caitlin Gabriel in 2014's *The Library*. The production, directed by Oscar winner Steven Soderbergh, told the story of a survivor of a deadly high school shooting.

Chloe Grace Moretz at the May 2014 Cannes Film Festival.

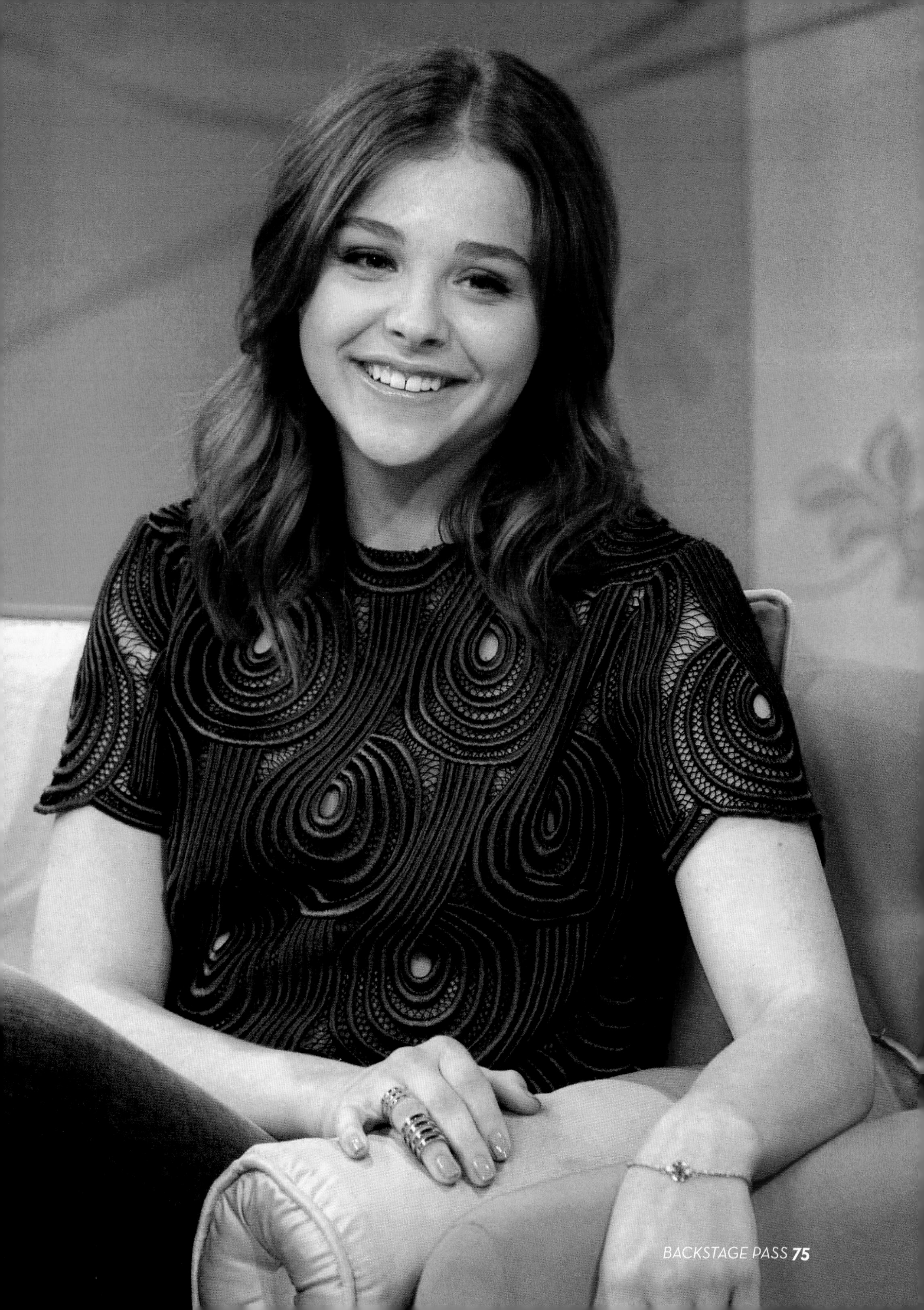

Like any good actress, Moretz takes film prep seriously. What may set her apart from the crowd, though, is that she doesn't just learn about issues, she becomes involved in them. While preparing for *The Equalizer*, for example, she visited Children of the Night, a Los Angeles-based organization dedicated to getting young girls off the streets. Chloe Grace befriended a number of young women at the shelter and still regularly returns to visit, often bearing gifts.

"You know as an actor they give you free clothes all the time? It's so stupid and I don't want any of them; I don't need the clothes," she told *The (UK) Independent* in October 2014. "If you're giving them to an actor who can buy their own clothes, go give them to a shelter! So every time I get boxes, I don't even open the boxes. I just take them straight to the shelter and go, 'Here you go, here's your stuff, because this is not what I need. I just do my job. I don't deserve that.'"

When it comes to doing good deeds and staying on the straight and narrow, Chloe Grace isn't just talking the talk, she's actually walking the walk. Despite more than a decade in the business, she's kept her career scandal free. She credits her family's support for keeping her grounded.

"If I wanted to go crazy, I would be doing it right now," she said during a 2014 press conference for *Clouds of Sils Maria*, noting that many young actors were heavy into partying by the time they reached her age. "For me, I've never had the need to want to do that. If I could create a world where I just did my job, where I could just do that and not have to worry about promotion or parties or red carpets or anything... that would be great. Sadly, it doesn't work that way."

Chloe Grace Moretz smiles as she talks with the media during a press conference for her 2014 film The Equalizer.

CHAPTER NINE

Jennifer Lawrence

Charming. Refreshing. Witty. Unexpected. Engaging.

Those are the words reporters use to describe actress Jennifer Lawrence. It seems the Kentucky native is somewhat of an oddity in Hollywood: She is unafraid to be herself.

Vanity Fair editor Jim Windolf wrote in a 2013 profile of the superstar: "She is completely unguarded and uncensored" and went on to describe her as "a celebrity who sounded more like a human being than a well-coached witness."

Famous for her red-carpet photo-bombs, JLaw has won her way into the hearts of casting directors, costars and – most importantly – fans.

Jennifer was 14 when she convinced her mother to take her to New York City so that she could audition and meet agents. She saw her share of rejection, but soon began to earn small roles. She realized enough success that her family moved to Los Angeles to support her dreams. Once there, she earned roles in a made-for-TV movie called *Company Town*, in a 2006 episode of *Monk*, and on *Cold Case* and *Medium* in 2007 and 2008, respectively.

Eventually, Jennifer landed a role on the TBS sitcom *The Bill Engvall Show*, in which she played the comedian's teenage daughter, Lauren Pearson.

"*The Bill Engvall Show*, I'm so grateful for it," she told *Under the Radar* magazine

Jennifer Lawrence attends The Hunger Games: Catching Fire *premiere in London.*

ALL ACCESS

Full name: Jennifer Shrader Lawrence

Birthdate: August 15, 1990

Birthplace: Louisville, Kentucky

Early jobs: Jennifer got her start in acting in 2007, when she landed the part of teenager Lauren Pearson in the TBS series *The Bill Engvall Show*. She won a 2009 Young Artist Award for her work on the show.

Big break: Critics took notice when Jennifer played the lead role in 2010's *Winter's Bone*. Her work earned her both Academy Award and Golden Globe nominations.

No go: Even superstars are told NO – on occasion. Before landing the part of Katniss in *The Hunger Games*, Jennifer auditioned for three now-iconic roles. She tried out for the role of Lisbeth Salander in *The Girl With The Dragon Tattoo* which ultimately went to Rooney Mara, Bella Swan in *Twilight* which went to Kristin Stewart, and Jules in *Superbad*, a part that went to Emma Stone.

Latest project: Jennifer stars in the final two films of the *Hunger Games* series, released in November 2014 and slated for release in November 2015, and she also has a cameo role in *Dumb and Dumber To*. Her first producer credit comes with *Glass Castle*, a film in which she'll also star. Other upcoming JLaw film projects: *Burial Rites, East of Eden, Ends of the Earth, X-Men Apocalypse* and *Joy*.

Twitter: Jennifer is anti-social media. She told *The Daily Beast* in November 2012: "Everybody was talking yesterday about Twitter and Instagram and Tumblr. It was really confusing me and overwhelming me. I literally started losing my breath. … I know by the time I get it, it'll be something else. I bought a CD case less than a year ago."

Reputation: She's an eccentric spirit who loves to laugh.

Why we love her: How can you not love a girl who sneaks beef jerky snacks into the Oscars?

in June 2010. "I had so much fun on that show, and we all became like family. It funded my indie career, so I could do the movies that I want."

While working on *Engvall*, Lawrence landed her first lead role in a film. She played a teenager growing up in a troubled household in 1970s Iowa in the 2008 movie *Poker House*. Her work won an award for "Best Performance" at the Los Angeles Film Festival.

As she earned larger roles, the young actress earned greater acclaim. She starred in *The Burning Plain*, a 2008 movie about a troubled teenager who accidentally murders her mother and her mother's boyfriend and then moves to Mexico. She won the Marcello Mastroianni award for emerging actors at the Venice Film Festival for that portrayal. In 2010's *Winter's Bone*, she played the part of Ree Dolly, a young girl fighting for survival in the mountains of West Virginia. The role earned her an Oscar nomination.

In the years since, Jennifer has continued to land high-impact, high-profile roles. She starred in 2011's *The Beaver* with Mel Gibson and Jodie Foster, and as Mystique in *X-Men: First Class*.

In 2012, she became Katniss, the lead in *The Hunger Games*, a film adaptation of Suzanne Collins' young adult novel. The film broke box-office records on opening weekend, and Lawrence was asked to reprise her role in subsequent films from the franchise: *The Hunger Games: Catching Fire* released in 2013, *The Hunger Games: Mockingjay – Part 1* released in November

2014 and *The Hunger Games: Mockingjay – Part 2* set for release in November 2015.

As if all that wasn't enough, Jennifer's other 2012 movies included *House at the End of the Street* with Elizabeth Shue, and two dramas with Bradley Cooper: *The Falling* and *Silver Linings Playbook*. Her outstanding work in *Silver Linings Playbook* helped fill her trophy case with awards including an Oscar, a Critics Choice Movie Award, an Independent Spirit Award, a Screen Actors Guild Award and a Golden Globe Award.

In 2013, she went on to star in *The Devil You Know* and *American Hustle*, for which she received an Academy Award nomination. She became the youngest actress ever to receive three Oscar nominations.

With paparazzi tracking her every move, casting directors vying for her time and her face adorning the covers of countless entertainment and fashion magazines each month, you'd think success might go to Jennifer's head. It hasn't.

"I've never understood why people have to become brats when they become successful," she told *The (London) Telegraph* in 2013. "I think you should work harder when you become successful because people are expecting more from you."

Following her own advice, Jennifer continues to work hard. Her other recent projects included the Depression-era drama *Serena* and she reprised her role as super villain Mystique in the film *X-Men: Days of Future Past*.

She's also starring in and producing *The Rules of Inheritance*, a film adaptation of the memoir of the same name by Claire Bidwell Smith about the hardships she went through when both of her parents were diagnosed with cancer when she was 14. She's set to star as Cathy Ames, who became one of the defining female antagonists of the 20th century, in the film adaptation of John Steinbeck's novel *East of Eden*. She's been cast in *Burial Rites*, a feature adaptation of Hannah Kent's novel centering on a murder trial in Iceland in 1829; in the love story *The Ends of the Earth;* and in the film adaption of New York Times best-seller *The Glass Castle*. Also on tap: *Joy*, a fact-based portrayal of Joy Mangano, the inventor of the Miracle Mop.

As she breathes life and breadth into some of the world's most famous charac-ters, Jennifer insists that she's still a little uncomfortable dealing with all the fanfare.

"Because I feel normal I expect to be treated normally and I'm trying to be patient with the fact that that's not exactly how everybody else feels," she told *The (London) Telegraph* in December 2013. "When I'm at the dentist getting my teeth cleaned, people are standing looking through the door. And I'm like, 'What would you do if someone was staring at you while you were getting your teeth cleaned?'

"It's a work in progress. When I meet young fans I understand them because I was like that too, but it's the real life day-to-day run-ins with people who sometimes don't really know how to act that make me feel weird, and I don't like it."

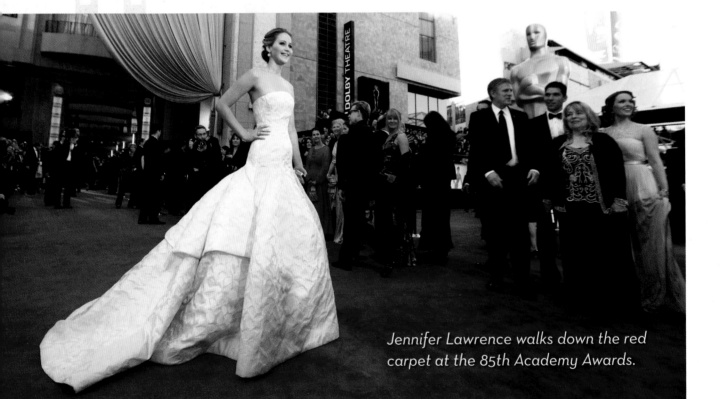

Jennifer Lawrence walks down the red carpet at the 85th Academy Awards.

CHAPTER TEN

Liam Hemsworth

Actor Liam Hemsworth has great news for fans: His *Hunger Games* character, Gale Hawthorne, will play a much more substantial role in the franchise's final two movies, both of which are based on *Mockingjay*, the last book in Suzanne Collins' popular science fiction adventure trilogy. In *Mockingjay*, as the revolt against the tyrannical Capitol spreads, Gale is determined to help his people by all means necessary – even violence.

"Gale is a big part of ... the big uprising," promises Liam.

While he may not be the outright star of *The Hunger Games*, the movies – the first of which was released on March 23, 2012 – catapulted him to a kind of fame that most others only dream of.

Of course, *The Hunger Games* can claim only partial credit for Liam's celebrity status. His older brothers, Luke and Chris, are also actors. And let's face it, when your brother – Chris – is famous for playing superhero "Thor," people tend to sit up and take notice.

As if the sibling connection wasn't enough, Liam's on-again, off-again relationship with singer Miley Cyrus, brought him considerable attention – much of it unwanted. The two met in the summer of 2009 while working on a movie, got engaged in May 2012 and called off their engagement in September 2013.

Liam's clearly not a fan of the paparazzi

ALL ACCESS

Full name: Liam Hemsworth

Birthdate: January 13, 1990

Birthplace: Melbourne, Australia

Early jobs: Liam attended his first audition when he was 16 and landed his first acting jobs in 2007, with guest appearances on the shows *Home and Away* and *McLeod's Daughters.* Soon he landed a recurring role on an Australian soap opera called *Neighbours.*

Good DNA: Liam isn't the only one in his family to make it big in show business; his brothers Chris and Luke are actors too. Middle child Chris is best known for his role as *Thor*; he headlines the cast of *Blackhat,* a cybercrime thriller scheduled for release in early 2015. Oldest brother Luke got his start on Australia's soap opera *Neighbours* (yes, the same show Liam later worked on). He stars in the 2014 movie *The Anomaly.*

Big break: Liam's big break in the United States came in 2010, when he was cast in *The Last Song.* In the film, he played Will Blakelee, a mechanic who falls in love with Ronnie Miller, played by actress/singer Miley Cyrus. The two actors started an off-screen romance and announced their engagement in 2012; they broke up in 2013.

Latest project: Liam's films *Hunger Games: Mockingjay - Part 1* and *Cut Bank* were released in late 2014. His fourth *Hunger Games* movie, *Mockingjay - Part 2* is due out in 2015. The Aussie actor is also set to star in 2015's thriller *By Way of Helena* with Woody Harrelson and the drama *The Dressmaker* with Kate Winslet.

On Twitter: @LiamHemsworth

Twitter followers: 983,000

Reputation: Reluctant heartthrob

Why we love him: He survived a very public breakup with Miley Cyrus and emerged from the relationship "more centered and grounded."

attention and tabloid coverage he received during and immediately after their break up, telling *Nylon Guys* magazine in 2014: "You never get used to it because you get followed and you get chased and it's never a fun experience. I think when people see photos of you out and about in your personal life, they assume that you've asked for it or that you want that attention, but I don't think anyone in their right mind asks for that kind of thing."

Still, he says he doesn't regret his relationship with the "Wrecking Ball" singer, insisting the pair will "always be best friends."

Fans know that, while family connections and a famous girlfriend may have increased Liam's name recognition, the handsome young actor has talent aplenty.

Liam was born in Melbourne, Australia, and his family moved to the small beach town of Philip Island when he was in high school. Inspired by his brothers' successes, Liam hired an agent and had his first successful audition when he was 16 years old, winning a small role on the Australian soap opera *Home and Away*. That was followed by another guest part on the TV series *McLeod's Daughters*.

In 2007, Liam landed a role on the popular soap opera *Neighbours*, playing paraplegic Josh Taylor, opposite his brother Luke, who'd been a regular on the show since 2000. In 2008, Liam won another role alongside his brother; the two worked on a children's television show called *The Elephant Princess*. Liam later had a role

Liam Hemsworth presents a Hunger Games moment at the 2014 MTV Movie Awards.

on TV's *Satisfaction*, starred in the British movie *Triangle*, and had a small part in the 2009 movie *Knowing* alongside actors Nicholas Cage and Rose Byrne.

In 2009, Liam moved to the United States to screen test for the title role in the movie *Thor*. He lost that part to his brother, but landed one of the leads in the coming-of-age romantic drama *The Last Song*. It was during the filming of this movie that Liam began dating his co-star – Miley – in real life. Aside from love, the film helped Liam win a Teen Choice Award and a Young Hollywood Award for "Breakthrough of the Year" and propelled him further up the Hollywood ladder.

In 2012, Liam landed two huge roles: the part of Gale in *The Hunger Games* and Billy the Kid in the action film *The Expendables 2* with Sylvester Stallone, Bruce Willis and Arnold Schwarzenegger. Liam said it was an honor to work with such action icons, particularly since he'd idolized them as a young boy.

"It was weird at first, you have to pinch yourself every once in a while," he told *Entertainment Weekly* in April 2012. "I was working with all these guys I grew up watching – it was nuts. Once Jean-Claude (Van Damme) kicked me in the chest by

Liam Hemsworth arrives on the red carpet for the world premiere of Hunger Games: Catching Fire.

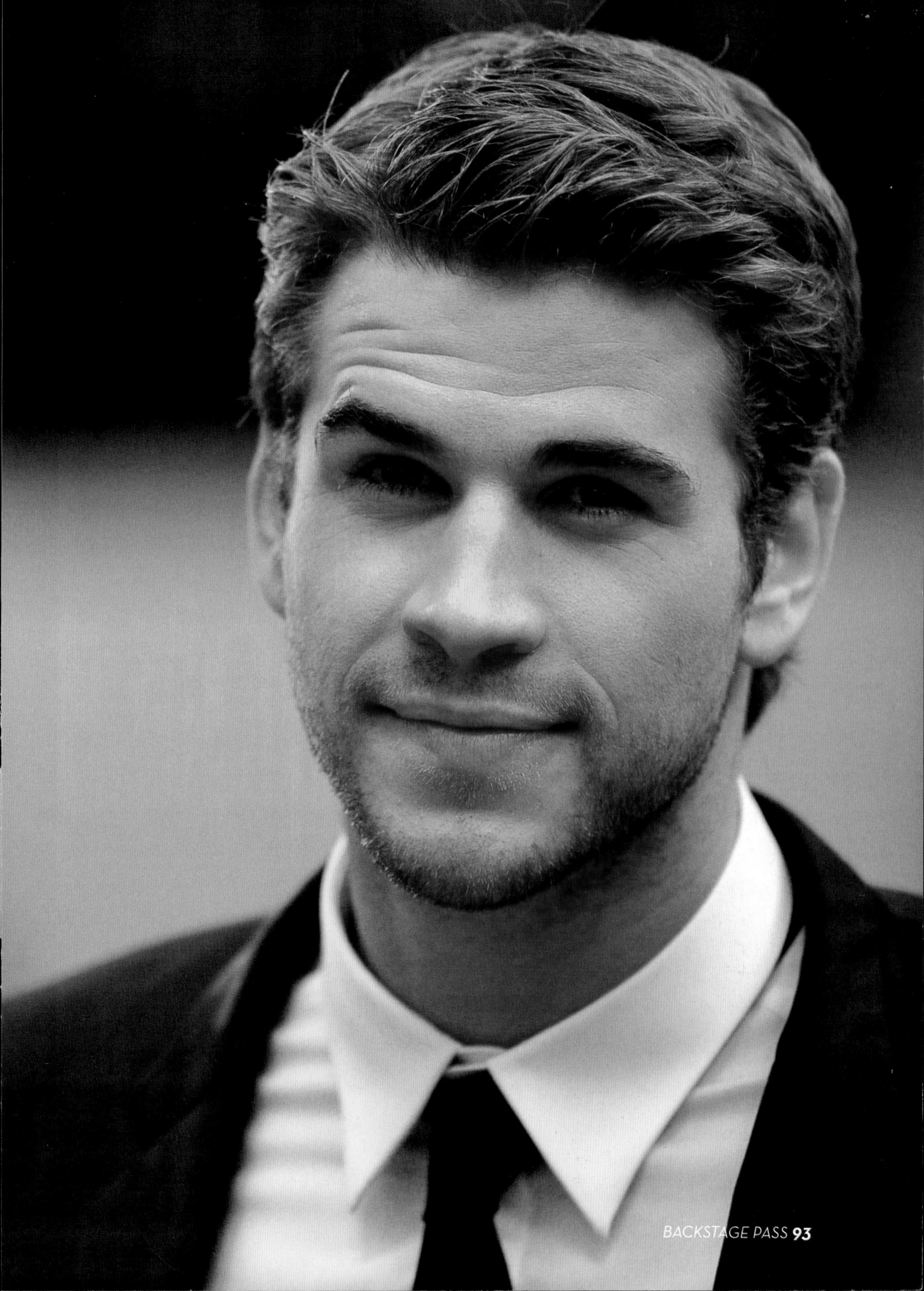

Liam Hemsworth arrives at the August 2013 U.S. premiere of Paranoia at DGA Theatre in West Hollywood, Calif.

accident. It was like a present, one of the most awesome kicks you could ever receive."

More movie roles have brought with them more opportunities to work with – and learn from – some of Hollywood's most iconic actors. In 2013, Liam starred with Gary Oldman and Harrison Ford in the corporate espionage thriller *Paranoia*, with Dwayne Johnson and Emma Roberts in the crime drama *Empire State*, and with Jennifer Lawrence and Josh Hutcherson in the second installment of *The Hunger Games* franchise.

Actor Billy Bob Thornton was complimentary when talking about the work he did with Liam on the 2014 thriller *Cut Bank*.

"He was great, what a great kid, I love him, we had a great time together up there," Thornton told *The West Australian* in April 2014. "He's a very focused kid when

he's acting, he was really focused and very good. I went out with him a couple of times and he and I just hit it off. As a matter of fact, he and I text each other all the time."

In addition to *Cut Back*, *Hunger Games: Mockingjay – Part 1* was released in late 2014. His fourth *Hunger Games* movie, *Mockingjay – Part 2* is due out in 2015.

The Aussie actor is also set to star in 2015's Western thriller *By Way of Helena* with Woody Harrelson and the drama *The Dressmaker* with Kate Winslet and Isla Fisher.

With all his success, it's fitting to recall that Liam's Hollywood breakthrough was spurred on by sibling rivalry. "I saw my brother doing it," he told *Interview* magazine in 2010, "and I thought I could do it better."

Indeed, Liam, you've done alright.